A WALK THROUGH

CW01623201

It is a balmy evening in late October 1942. A fresh-faced youngster of eigheten waits patiently on the platform for the train that will take him to war in the Mediterranean and Far East.

As he puffs lazily on his 'Capstan', certain sights, sounds and smells recall events and episodes from an idyllic childhood together with memories of the friends, relatives and acquaintances who made it so.

Such is the background to *A Walk Through Frankwell Street* by Len Rowlands.

Frankwell Street, is, of course, in Tywyn and Len Rowlands is a Tywyn boy. If you were brought up in the town in the thirties and very early forties, then travel again with Len along the paths of memory lane when, as he says: 'The sun shone every day from cloudless blue skies'. He'll be glad of your company!

FRANKWELL STREET

Photo: Brad Banks

A Walk Through Frankwell Street

MEMORIES
OF
A TYWYN CHILDHOOD

Len Rowlands

Llawer o ddiolch
Am alw 'hwo'
Cofion fil
Len

GWASG GEE
DINBYCH (DENBIGH)

By the same author:

CHOELIAIS I FAWR (Gwasg Gee, 1993)

Printed by:
GEE & SON, DENBIGH

1939 - 1945

Dedicated
To the Memory of those with whom we
played, studied and worked and
who never made it home.

'For oft, when on my couch I lie
In vacant or in pensive mood,
They flash upon that inward eye
Which is the bliss of solitude: . . .'

— William Wordsworth, *The Daffodils*.

In compiling this volume I am deeply indebted to the kindness and good offices of:

Mrs. Brenda Webster, 'Tudor Court', Rhiwbina, Cardiff who not only typed my manuscript but also coped so valiantly with the Welsh place-names!

Gwasg Gee, Denbigh, for accepting this short memoir for publication when this press is usually preoccupied with far weightier tomes and Administrative Manager, Mr. T. Alun Williams, for his ever listening ear and timely advice.

And last, but by no means least, Mr. Brad Banks of: 'Foto Images', Tywyn for the cover picture of Frankwell Street (a little different now from that Autumn afternoon in 1942!)

Diolch yn fawr i gyd!

Preface

This book owes its existence to a Christmas card. It came from my old friend E.D. (Ian) Williams, late of 1 and 16, Idris Villas but now of 'Rose Cottage', Tregaron.

'Tywyn', he said, 'has changed beyond recognition: it is full of strange faces and unfamiliar landmarks.'

My mind raced back six decades to the closely-knit community I knew as a boy. 'Distance' they say 'lends enchantment' but I gave my imagination a free rein, and, during the early-year 'freeze-up' I tried to conjure up the sights sounds and smells of a Tywyn that seems to have passed into history: to a time when the sun shone brightly every day and we played under perpetually blue skies.

I decided then, in a moment of nostalgia, to commit my thoughts to paper and, perhaps, who knows, encourage others of my friends who, like myself, have now passed the milestone of 'three score years and ten' to remember in my company those long lost, happy, carefree days of yore before they vanish for ever from the memory.

Let me explain the title. First of all, when Tywyn was 'Tywyn on Sea' on the coloured posters decorating our stations up and down the country (together with 'Tails wagalot for Winalot' and 'Growing boys need Virol') each guide book featured Frankwell Street under the title 'Old Tywyn'

(Photographer Brand Banks of 'Foto Images' has recently opened my eyes to another Frankwell Street complete with state of the art decor and 'Sky' aerials!). Nevertheless, it is of course, old Frankwell Street in Old Tywyn complete with its eccentric, though friendly, characters that I have tried to remember in the pages that follow.

There is, however, a more poignant reason. On the afternoon of the day that I left the town to join the Royal Navy, I visited my friends, Mr. and Mrs. Leonard Roberts of 7, Red Lion Street.

I remembered the many happy hours I had spent in number 7. The purpose of my visit was always the same — to discuss my French and German homework with Eddie. However, there were distractions! Fred, a talented musician was only too happy to entertain us on the piano-accordion, and I always listened enthralled as he displayed his dexterity on those keys! Occasionally, there were youngsters present who used to hang on to Fred's every chord. It was obvious to all and sundry even in those far-off days where his final destiny lay.

Bobby Graham, although a decorated air-crew member of the RAF in later days, had a leaning towards the sea — perhaps through the influence of his maternal grandfather — and this was manifested in his love of building model ships. Quietly and patiently he would work in his small corner saying very little as he delicately picked up small bits of cord dipped in glue with his tweezers to form the intricate rigging of a Spanish Galleon. After many weeks of painstaking dedication to rigging, sails and hull, and carefully colourful painting, the vessel was ready for the display cupboard together with the rest of the Armada.

Sadly, Bobby Graham is one of those to whom this book is dedicated.

With an unfailing visit to Mr. Bill Graham's garden aviary a few doors away, time passed all too quickly and the given tasks of Caradog Williams and Edgar Jones were completely forgotten! Sometimes, I was invited to stay for supper — Johnny Morris' faggots and Mr. Roberts' home-grown peas were truly a mouth-watering combination! Other times, Eddie would accompany me to Latham's in National Street and we would feast the night away on fish, chips and 'Vimto' discussing our strategy for sweeping the board once again in the forthcoming Tywyn and Aberdovey carnivals as the comic duo Mutt and Jeff.

It was with these happy memories in mind that I went to bid farewell to Mr. and Mrs. Roberts that afternoon. Mr Roberts was far from well, his first-ever illness. 'As it is such a pleasant afternoon, Len' he said, 'would you like to take me for a walk through Frankwell Street as far as Pendre and back?' I readily consented. It was his last-ever walk in Tywyn, and mine, too, before leaving for war.

L.R. Cardiff, February 1996

I had always wanted to join the Royal Navy, especially after seeing those handsome sailors from HMS *Furious* and HMS *Resolution* swaying nonchalantly along the front at Aberystwyth with a pretty girl on each arm!

But now, standing on Tywyn station at ten to six on the evening of Tuesday, October 27th, 1942 waiting for the mail train to Shrewsbury, I wasn't too sure.

The apprehension had been aroused when I saw a photograph in one of the London papers. It depicted a towering ship's mast with numerous sailors like ants climbing up and down the rigging, and then at a given signal, holding fast with one arm and leg whilst thrusting the other arm and leg outwards to form the body into the letter 'K'.

I had seen the same thing done by the trapeze artistes at 'Chapman's Circus' at 'Morfa Bach' and my reaction was the same then! But at least, they had a layer of grass under them not a concrete parade ground!

No, I was never one for heights and I feared this aspect of my training far more than anything else. I recalled those halcyon summer evenings of the thirties when, at the invitation of Ifan Lewis, we had been invited to 'Y Faenol' to play football, and then to engage in a game of Cowboys and Indians. We gathered from all quarters, just like the gathering of the clans, from Frankwell Street, Athelestan Road, Cambrian Terrace, High Street, Gwalia and Idris Villas.

It was during one of those games of Cowboys and Indians

that I sought to evade my captors by the brilliant ploy of climbing up a ladder to the top of a hayrick in one of the barns. The trick worked but then it slowly dawned on me that what goes up must come down! Despite the jeering and cheering there was no coming down, and it was only when Ifan suggested leaving me there all night to the rats, mice, bats and other creatures of the night that I made my unsteady descent. It wasn't until I reached 'Clawddbras' however that my legs ceased shaking with fright!

Would I be the object of derision during playtime in 'Pen-y-bryn' school the following day after my evening's exploits? I spent a sleepless night, and undertook a slow, ponderous walk to school hoping that my cycle trip to the Co-op and back to Idris Villas would have made me late, and I wouldn't have to go. But it didn't.

When I got to school I noticed that the boys had far more important things than me to think about. They were carrying cardboard boxes under their arms, the contents of which would be revealed at playtime.

The boxes contained games which they had constructed at home with the prime purpose of collecting as many cigarette cards as possible for 'charging' so many cards 'a go' and offering those self-same cards as prizes to the winners.

Some had constructed boards on which there were hooks each with a number and for two cigarette cards one could have three small rubber hoops to throw at the board. If one of the hoops landed on the hook containing the number six, then six cigarette cards were his.

Others had boards set out in squares on which there was a number. By throwing a penny, one could for two cigarette cards, see how many cards were his if the coin landed on a square without touching the dividing lines.

One or two used marbles, carried in the pocket. A large glass marble was placed on the ground and for two cigarette cards three smaller marbles were given. For each one that scored a direct hit on the large one a prize of one cigarette card was given.

A simple device was the one whereby holes with numbers were made in the lid of a shoe box and for two cigarette cards a small rubber ball was issued, the idea being to get the ball into those holes containing the larger numbers for a prize of as many cards as possible.

There were home-made boards containing covered squares by way of a 'lucky dip'. You invested two cigarette cards to unveil a square. Sometimes the square contained a zero; other times ten, and one proudly walked away with ten cigarette cards!

Those not interested in games of chance gathered by the small wall that divided us from the Infant School to be entertained by Rob Jones the butcher and his glove-puppet 'Ollie'. Rob composed some exceptionally humorous scripts for the dialogue between himself and 'Ollie' and one wishes that he had lived in the days of children's television.

'All good things come to an end' says the old adage, and soon the fun was over as 'Gron' (Goronwy Idris Williams) rang the bell and summoned us all into our class-lines for the last lesson of the morning. As we trooped into the cloak-room and into the hall I shouted to Ronald Owen: 'Don't forget, Frankwell Street are playing Idris Villas in the Cup on Saturday!' A glare came from 'Gron' followed by: 'Remember empty vessels make the most din!'

By lunch-time, however, all was forgiven for 'Gron' was going to marry Miss Edwards of Standard Five and coming to live to Idris Villas, and so, living in Idris Villas myself, my services as an errand boy were required. (The same happened when I was at the County. Going home for lunch, T. V. Davies would now and again forget his glasses and, as I lived a few doors away from Mr. and Mrs. T.V., I would be dispatched during first lesson to get them).

But back to 'Gron'. Sometimes, however, I would 'avoid his gaze' as the Good Book says because I wanted to race Bob Clarke Roberts to the Post Office. There, Miss Davies and Miss Evans were on the look-out for us to arrive so that we could deliver the telegrams that had come in during the morning. For delivery in the town, it was a penny half-penny but outside it was three pence, a veritable fortune! It was on one of these occasions that I learnt the words: 'Sinking fast'. Lewis Pugh was very ill in Athelestan Road and one of the children had sent a telegram which needed an answer. 'How is father?' queried the wire, I was given the answer 'Sinking fast' to take back to the Post Office.

Following the band also yielded some form of revenue in those far-off days. When 'On the march' it was rather silly to carry music stands and so when the Tywyn Silver Band under their able conductors R. O. Jones (later J. H. Markham) stood in a circle and played on the Marine Parade outside the Market Hall or in Corbett Square, we were recruited by the players to stand in front of them holding the music books with our two hands so that they rested on our forehead with the usual clothes peg holding the pages together should the wind blow from Cardigan Bay! The selections played were the usual for those days: 'Gems of Cambria'; 'The Lost Chord'; 'The William Tell Overture'; 'The Men of Harlech'; 'David of the White Rock'; 'In a Monastery Garden'; 'The Bluebells of Scotland'; 'Y Delyn Aur'; 'Crug-y-bar and other tear-jerking Welsh hymns. (We who were in Standard Five and Six in the Junior

School in 1937 have good reason to remember 'Y Delyn Aur'. We were part of the vast National Eisteddfod Choir in Machynlleth conducted by Mr. Bumford Griffiths of Cardiff when Sir Howell Williams, a London Welsh philanthropist, was so thrilled by our rendering of the hymn that he gave us all a silver cup in memory of the event. In the pre-war years, it was difficult in Tywyn not to find a mantelpiece without a silver cup!)

I was usually pounced upon by Griffith Jones, Rennie's grandfather, if I had not been 'booked' by the two euphonium players Ivor Roberts the baker and my grandfather. The penny or tuppence reward came in very handy when Tom Mander's Amusements were at 'Morfa Bach' or indeed in Ivor's own shop usually open late opposite that local outpost of American civilisation — the cinema!

(These were, of course, the days before the two bands, known respectively as the 'wet' band and the 'dry' band. The schism arose when certain players wanted to finish the practice a little earlier to slip the few yards across National Street from the Church House to the 'Tredegar' before closing time. A vote was taken and the consensus of opinion came down in favour of the 'Status Quo' thus making way for the split and the formation of the two bands.

The 'wet' band found an able conductor in the talented musician, Jack Jarman, who was equally at home fronting both a brass-band and a mixed choir. In his younger days in the town, Mr. Jarman had a rhythm group called 'Jack Jarman's Syncopated Band'. Tywyn people, being what they were, called it 'Jack Jarman's Constipated Band'!

(It was Mr. Jarman's eldest son Willie, now 'lying in some corner of a foreign field' who first took me school. I was, of course, under age, and, having a penny to spend one Summer lunch-time, I made my way up Idris Villas to Miss Graham's tuck-shop opposite the station. Having bought my sweets, I wandered as far as Athelestan Road, and there, sitting on the wall in the sunshine I began to eat. Suddenly, Willie appeared obviously on his way somewhere. 'Where are you going, Will?' I shouted 'to school' he replied. 'You can have a sweet if I can come with you' I ventured. No sooner had I asked my question than Willie was over digging into my bag of sweetmeats. I jumped down from the wall and made my way with Willie past the County, the slate-wharf where my grandfather worked, past 'Trefri', 'Brynhyfryd', 'Brynteg' and eventually to the Infant School where all the pupils were playing under the watchful eyes of Mrs. Jones the 'Head' and Miss Edwards. If I expected a warm welcome, I was disappointed! They pointed my nose in the direction of the gate and my lonely walk home without Willie. I made my way to the Cottage Hospital and sat on a seat. Suddenly I heard the 'chug-chug' of a motor-bike coming from the direction of Aberdovey. It was Mr. Morris the Gas who would be passing number 18, Idris Villas! He stopped and realised that a four year-old shouldn't be wandering on his own that far from home. He crossed the road, picked me up and put me to sit on his tool-bag in the side-car, and delivered me safely to 'Gwernol'. It was the first of many rides I was to have on Mr. Morris' lumpy tool bag over the years that I spent in 'Pen-y-Bryn'.)

Yet another means of making a copper or two was to wash the 'Head's' car. W. Pryce-Williams had a 'Rover', and, probably because I went to 'Bethel' where Mr. Williams was deacon, I was made 'foreman' and asked whether I would like sixpence myself or to appoint an assistant for three-pence each, or, indeed, to appoint another three for a penny half-penny each! With my mind on the future of Idris Villas in the Street

Cup (one of my grandmother's egg-cups covered in silver paper) I thought carefully; a short list would have to be drawn up! Who were the good players I could recruit to play for us when they themselves were not engaged? My mind's eye scanned the town — Eldon Roberts from the High Street? 'W.O.' (William Owen) Davies, Rennie Lloyd (Lewis) and Tegwyn Jones from Cambrian Terrace? What about Neville Roberts from Athelestan Road or Cyril Wyn (Harries) from 'Y Llain'? At a pinch perhaps I could tempt Ronald Owen and his brother 'Dei Bach': I had some serious thinking to do!

Most of the games were played in the field next to the Dysynni Wharf — despite the slope. Looking back, I admire the patience of Mrs. E. T. Williams, Edgar's mother, and indeed his grandmother, whose scullery window more or less bordered on the field. Throughout the afternoon, there would be a long queue — yes, we learnt to queue long before war came — for cups of cold water, and sad to say, some put more effort into their drinking than they did into their game!

The 'Street Cup' in those days was ranked practically on par with the 'Peake Ramsey' cup which was played for in the evenings around Easter after the change of the hour. The 'Peake Ramsey', named after a local celebrity, brought together teams from most of the Dysynni Valley villages — Abergynolwyn, Bryncrug, Llanegryn, Llwyngwril, Rhoslefain, and, what was also fascinating were the teams bearing such names as 'King Kong' (a team of veterans, once well-known local players) and the 'Dinky Doos' named after characters from a Hollywood film. The teams were composed of local players, some, in fairness with 'Cambrian Coast' and 'Mid-Wales' experience. Abergynolwyn recruited from the Royal Navy in the person of

Ivor Fielding[1] — a blonde bombshell who tore down the wing like the proverbial 'white tornado'! A gifted player who played several representative matches, I regarded Ivor as the best locally-produced player of all time. (Forty years later, talking to one of the Cardiff City 'greats' Jack Evans — 'the Bala Bang' — I was informed when I told him I came from Tywyn of one Huw 'Erwporthor' who was well-known in North Wales in his day, rather like my namesake, Len Rowlands ('Toxy') was after the War. Thinking of Welsh-speaking Jack Evans, how many league players today find themselves on the park on Saturday afternoon and in the 'set-fawr' on Sunday? Strangely enough, I never met Cardiff City's greatest player at Ninian Park but I did as a thirteen-year-old in Tywyn when Fred Keenor, Captain of the 1927 F.A. Cup winners, 'guested' for Tywyn against Aberdovey. As I saw him signing autographs that Summer evening, I little dreamt that I one day would have the pleasure of teaching his grand-daughter, Valerie. . . .
. . . .

I looked at my watch; Five to Six I lit a 'Capstan' — the sailor's cigarette. To me, a 'Player' had always been the sailor's cigarette with the imposing figure of the blue jacket from HMS *Hero* on the front with his 'full set' in glorious array. But one day, catching the two o'clock back to Tonfannau, my travelling companion was Gwilym Roberts, 'Gwilym the Nurse' because his mother was the local District Nurse. Gwilym, although later commissioned, was a 'DEMS' gunner — sailors from the Royal Navy who had been delegated to Merchant ships to man the guns. It was considered a 'cushy' number because there were no parades, no falling in, no routine, no regimentation and always the best of food. Another local 'DEMS' was

[1] At the time of writing, Commander Fielding is still alive and spending his days in a West Country nursing home.

Alfie Roberts (Jack Roberts the barber's brother). Alas, they like their colleagues in the other branches of the service suffered heavy casualties during the 'U Boat' offensive. When I travelled with Gwilym his ship was in Liverpool's Gladstone Dock and, for anyone travelling north the two o'clock to Barmouth Junction was the favourite.

Gwilym sat in the corner of the compartment and I could see the 'pine-end' of his twenty cigarettes with the words: 'H.M. Ships Only' in his jacket, just under his left arm-pit. He saw me looking 'Do you Smoke?' he asked offering me what I found out to be a 'Capstan' 'Thank you' I replied taking one. 'Yes', he went on 'this is the sailor's cigarette. I wouldn't smoke anything else.' By the time I reached Tonfannau I had been converted: from now on I would be a 'Capstan' smoker too!

The Small Heath, Birmingham firm of C. W. Bryant and Son had brought work for hundreds in the area, and indeed, for many outside, as they built the anti-aircraft establishment at Tonfannau. I, too, found work in the office after leaving school, for the princely sum of ten shillings a week (50p)! I had three duties to perform. The main one was visiting Mr. Matheson, the Canteen Manager, to ask what he had in mind for the chocolate and cigarettes ration for that particular week. (This was at a time when both cigarettes and chocolate were difficult to come by in town shops but Bryant workers were assured of both in small measure each week.) I then went back to the office, sat in my corner, and then produced a rubber stamp, an ink pad, and a small but thick writing pad. In this way, I first of all stamped out some five or six hundred coupons, some three on a page, and then carefully cut them all out with a pair of scissors. I then filled each one in. 'This coupon' went the finished product 'entitles the holder to purchase forty cigarettes and two bars of chocolate at the Canteen.' I then proudly took my masterpieces through the corridor to the Wages Office where, on Friday, the willing hands who filled the wage packets with the workers' just deserts added my 'piece de resistance' for good measure!

My second task was to walk around the site to visit the foremen and collect the National Savings money which I would take back to the office to be converted into stamps. I would then retrace my steps back to the site offices to deliver 'the goods'. It was, however, the third task which I valued the most. It was a trip to Tywyn between trains to buy tobacco for Mr. Baggs the materials' clerk. Not only did these trips give me a good leg stretch, they also took me out of the office to visit Mr. J. H. Markham or Mr. George Benford. I also found time to visit 18, Idris Villas for a cold drink in Summer and hot coffee in Winter.

By this time, I was also in uniform as a member of 'B' Company of the Third Mermont Battalion of the Home Guard which was commanded by Major T. R. Rowlands, and, on parade nights, I couldn't get home soon enough to change. I used to collect milk after tea from 'Plas-y-Bryn' and I always went in uniform so that I could practise my salutes as R.A.F.s officers from Morfa Camp made their way through Idris Villas to the Corbett Arms Hotel for dinner and a drink.

Yes, I was proud of my Home Guard uniform and I kept it as neatly and as tidily as I could. I was the only member of the Company to wear a special badge on the sleeve of my left arm — blue and red, it consisted of a Crown with the letters 'R.N.Y.E.', one letter in each corner. The badge meant that I was a 'Y' entrant for the Royal Navy. It was a scheme whereby holders of a School Certificate with service in one of the Cadet forces or Home Guard was ear-marked for a commission. (Am I going to be honest? Yes, I am — I didn't get one!)

I loved turning up at the Market Hall to pick up a rifle for parades at the Drill Hall, normally taken by Sgt. Major Jack Lloyd, a local man and a First World War veteran who was a member of the T.A., now in the Army but seconded to the Home Guard. Those of us younger members occasionally had our own parades at the Market Hall itself, just below the clock-tower, where we were instructed in the military art of signalling. Our instructor was Mr. H. Harwood Thompson, a retired bank official who lived in Cleveland Avenue. When out on exercises, we were expected to show what Mr. Thompson had taught us.

On the odd Sunday afternoon we would march down to Penllyn to the butts at the rifle range. Despite the fact that I was a fairly decent marksman I was chosen as a marker — perhaps the others needed more practice! But I was happy to signal 'bull', 'magpie', 'Outer' and so on. After such escapades there was little time to change for evening service at 'Bethel' and so I used to go in uniform, and as I walked in I could see the 'old sweats' from local camps in the gallery mouthing; 'He's a bit young, isn't he?

My youthful countenance in uniform did, I must admit, on one occasion, cause me a great deal of embarrassment. On the odd Sunday evening, I used to put my uniform on after church and proceed to what we called 'the Aerodrome' which was in reality the R.A.F. Camp at Sandilands. There, around eight o'clock they projected a film which was free for servicemen. During the week, I used to call at the guard-room by the main gate and request details of Sunday's film. If the title took my fancy, I would go along.

This particular Sunday, however, it was an 'ENSA' show. As

part of their war effort, stars of screen, stage and radio would devote part of their time to entertaining the troops both at home and abroad under the banner of 'ENSA'. Occasionally, the 'show' would consist of only three people — a very well proportioned pianist, an elderly violinist and an opera singer whose better days lay in the past! This, however, was a fully 'blown' variety show. During the performance, a scantily-clad blonde came down from the stage, took my hand, and led me to a chair where she sat on my lap, sang a line of 'You made me love you!', then kissed me, sang another line and kissed me again until, at the end of the song my face was a tattoo of red lips! I didn't mind so much being embarrassed in front of servicemen, but on that particular evening there were local celebrities who knew me so well present, and it was to be a long time before I would live the incident down!

Once a fortnight we had to do an all-night duty, the idea being that should an invasion take place we would go around the houses waking up members of the Company to call them to arms. As far as I know, this never happened but from time to time we would be tested by H.Q. in Welshpool or Newtown. On one of these duties my two companions were Hughie Jones, 'Tyddyn-Du' and Peter Williams 'Pendre' who occupied the two armchairs around the fireplace after the usual 'brew up' and cakes provided free. I went to sleep on the floor on a couple of army blankets covered by my greatcoat.

Hughie, who was a baker, left early in the morning and so did his companion who had to fire one of the engines on the Tal-y-Llyn railway. The next thing I remembered were eight hefty strokes above my head! Eight o'clock! I had an hour to walk home, wash, shave, change, have breakfast, jump on my 'trusty steed' in order to present myself in the office in Tonfannau by nine o'clock!

It only happens in the best of Ealing comedies but it happened to me — I came face to face with the C.O., on his way to work.

'Wha are you doing in uniform at this time of the morning?' asked T.R., as I 'chopped off' a salute despite the fact that he was not wearing his major's crown.

'I'm sorry, Sir' I blurted, 'I've been on all night duty and I slept late!'

'Slept?' he replied 'slept?' only then did I realise what a stupid answer I had given!

That incident, however, did not prevent him from giving me a glowing testimonial to present to their Lords Commissioners of the Admiralty.

> (I have known Leonard Rowlands for many years, in fact since childhood. I have always found him very intelligent, industrious, and of good address. He has served under me in the Home Guard for 12 months, and during this time he has been very attentive to his duties, punctual in attendance, and takes very great delight in all appertaining to military matters. I can highly recommend him for appointment to the navy, and he will no doubt prove a credit to all.)
>
> (*signed*) T. R. Rowlands Major (O/C B. Coy)

It was events such as this that made me sad to leave the Home Guard together with my companions young and old. I looked back happily at those parades for 'War Weapons Week' when we joined the Army, the Navy, the Air Force and the other Auxiliary Services to march through the town trying to 'out do' our regular comrades. Then there were the Armistice Day parades which took me for the first time to Tywyn's ancient St. Cadvan's Church containing the famous 'St. Cadvan's

Stone' from the Seventh Century bearing the oldest inscription in the Welsh language and also the effigy of Gruffydd ap Adda of Dolgoch whose eyes water at the sign of rain.

Another curio worth noting was that just across the road from the Market Hall in the front bar of the 'Tredegar Arms' which I noticed for the first time when detailed to buy a flagon or two for my thirsty comrades on duty one Bank Holiday. It was a painting in a circle around the ceiling light which depicted four sour-faced, even sinister, local faces, their chins pointing towards the centre said to have been painted about the middle of the Nineteenth Century by a wandering French artist for a few tankards of ale. At one time (during the reign of Joseph Owens) it was said that there was no need for 'mine host' to shout: 'Time, gentlemen please!' in the 'Tred' because when the patrons noticed the 'old boys winking at them, they left of their own accord! Yes, despite my Grammar School education, without the Home Guard I would be sadly lacking in these interesting touches of local history!

I entered Tywyn Grammar School (The County) in September 1937 walking proudly up Station Road my new satchel shining in the morning sun and wishing a cheery 'Morning Fred!' to Frederick Roberts who worked at that time in the office of Griffith Davies and Son, Agricultural Merchants. Within a few minutes I would be joining Fred's brother, Eddie, to walk through the sacred portals of 'Brynarfor'. From that moment we were destined to be form-mates for the next four years, for most of the time sitting together.

Within two years, the satchel, by this time slightly the worse for wear, was joined on its journeys to and from Idris Villas by a gas-mask. At first, it was a cardboard-box carried over the shoulder by a length of string. But soon I was the envy of the Form as it was carried in a spanking new linen case — a gift from my employer — J. D. Jones of 'Pretoria Buildings'. Catching me running home one day while I was still in 'Pen-y-Bryn', he asked me to post some letters, and from then on I became his gwâs bach, his 'dog's body' in my leisure hours at his drapery business.

On Friday evenings I walked to Pant-y-Neuadd (which Mr. Jones called Pant-y-Nefoedd) to fetch milk and butter, (As I turned left off the Aberdovey road to walk the tree-lined avenue to the dairy I looked at the deserted fields on either side and recalled those Libral Party Rallies of the early thirties when the whole area thronged with visitors. Sponsored by the then Member of Parliament for Merioneth, Mr. (later Sir) Henry Haydn Jones, the rallies were an interesting and exciting day out. Held in Summer, in the best of weather, members of the Liberal Party travelled from all over the County to be present and to take part in the various activities that made the day the success it was. There were exhibitions and demonstrations, stalls selling home-made cakes, knitted garments, ornaments, plants and flowers, ice-cream, and, for mischievous children, those tubes of 'toothpaste' filled with water that could be squirted over friend and foe! There were also the usual amusements which we associated with Tom Mander and Henry Studd — shooting galleries, coconut shies, rolling pennies and 'hoop-las'. Grabbing our attention were the conjurers, fire-eaters, mind-readers and fortune tellers not forgetting George Childlow from Abergynolwyn in his loin cloth tattooed from head to toe as well as the many refreshment tents with their mouth-watering titbits. Music was provided by the Silver bands of the Royal Oakley, Corris, and Tywyn. In the evening in the huge marquee provided for the purpose, the highlight of the day was a stupendous variety show. One of these, I remember, was compered by a delightful local character from Gwalia whose son was in school with me. For all the tea in China, I couldn't understand why the items he announced never appeared on the stage! 'And now', he said, 'from Tan-y-Grisiau we have Wilf Morris and his singing dogs'. An item surely to be savoured for a long time to come. Sadly, instead of the said Wilf Morris and his canine companions we had two portly gentlemen dressed as police constables who sang; 'The Two Gendarmes'! Later, I was told that our jovial compère couldn't read and the programme's running order meant nothing to him! Shortly after this he passed away and the family moved to South Wales.

Another of my duties in Pretoria was to post letters for Mrs. Jones to their son Dr. J. D. Jones, MRCS, LRCP, who was then a houseman at Chester's Royal Infirmary. With war clouds in the horizon, Dr. Jones, like many other local boys who were drawn to medicine, Dr Ranyl Rhydwen, Dr. Tom Tibbott-Davies, joined the Forces. I well remember after one leave, helping to carry John's cases to the station as he made his way back to his Field Hospital in France. As I put his cases down, he fumbled in his pockets for a few coins. 'Here we are, Leonard' he said 'thank you very much!' I made a bee-line to Annie Edwards' small tuck-shop opposite the station eager to spend my windfall only to find to my utter chagrin that they were French coins!

When provisions were called for, it was the short trip to Porthgwyn which I loved, not because the family were fellow-members in Bethel and Richie our organist but because of the permanent aroma of ground coffee which always made me think of an eastern bazaar. One day, Mrs. Jones ran short of toilet paper — not the usual roll but the single sheets in the oblong cardboard container. 'Leonard' she said 'run quickly to Porthgwyn to get me a toilet block!' Taking her at her word I did so. Skipping through the door I blurted: 'A toilet block for Mrs. Jones Pretoria, please!' Richie was standing there, immaculate, not a hair out of place, a collar and tie, and, despite the fact that he had just come from the bakehouse, there wasn't a speck of flour on his long, brown, overall. 'What do you want?' he asked, smiling as he did so. 'A toilet block for Mrs. Jones, Pretoria,' I repeated. 'Oh, you don't want us' he said 'you want Dick Hughes the pumber!'

From time to time, I caught Archie's 'Crossville' bus to Abergynolwyn to do a spot of debt collecting. Most of the time, however, I sat on a chair in the fitting-room within view of the door so that if a customer arrived when Mr. Jones was in the house having tea or out the back, I would ring the bell and politely inform the customer: 'Mr. Jones will be here now.'

Sometimes, what the customer wanted wasn't in stock and I would be dispatched across the road to the drapery business of Mr. Robert Ellis next to Tom Griffiths the barber with the words: 'Don't forget to ask for trade discount!' ringing in my ears.

After 'Pretoria', rather dark and dreary, established at the turn of the century, I found Mr. Ellis's shop a breath of fresh air — light, airy, clean and full of colour. But there, it was new. I well remembered that Saturday morning in the early thirties when I made my way to the station to take the ten o'clock train to Aberystwyth for our annual Sunday School trip looking in horror at Mr. & Mrs. Ellis's shop and home a smouldering ruin! As we stood on the platform where Harold Morris and Griffith Thomas loaded their goods for delivery and faced the shop directly opposite we were overtaken with pity to see half-burnt furniture, charred bedding, and still-smouldering suits. The sadness of the scene even cast a dark shadow over our day by the sea. It wasn't long, however, as we went around our daily tasks before we saw Mr. and Mrs. Ellis in a brand-new shop and house in the High Street. And the old premises? Rechristened 'Cremlyn', the flat became the comfortable home of Mr. & Mrs. H. T. Davies and the shop the high class ladies' hairdressing salon of 'Wenda' (the Misses B. and M. E. Davies).

My 'salary' in 'Pretoria' was 1/6 (7½p) a week paid on a Saturday evening (plus in cold weather a bowl of soup). The shilling I took home but the sixpence, I'm afraid, was spent on riotous living in Clay's on a bag of stale cakes!

Wednesday was Mr. Jones's half-day, and I would fetch his tin of maggots from Jones the Chemist, and he would cycle to the Broadwater to fish for trout or the mouth of the Dysynni to try his luck for bass. Any maggots left over were mine to try my luck for brown mountain trout in 'Caethle' brook, keeping a 'weather-eye peeled for Tommy Jones, who, although he had heard me reciting my verses dozns of times in 'Bethel', if he found me trespassing would send me away with a flea in my ear!

Fishing days, however, were few and far between when the evacuees arrived from Birkenhead. Their day of arrival was a very busy one, and, knowing the town well, Mr. T. V. Davies who was in charge of allocation asked me, amongst others, to present myself in the school hall in the very early evening to direct and escort these little strangers to their new homes. Refreshments were attractively laid out and most tempting for those of us who stood and waited! In 1941 whilst struggling with my 'Maths' paper for C.W.B., in that very hall, I could still smell their delicious aroma!

Eventually, somewhere between eight-thirty and nine, we heard the whistle of the train in the station, and we waited with eager anticipation for the long 'Crocodile' to slowly wind its way through the gates of 'Brynarfor' and eventually into the hall. Many looked tired and bedraggled rather like the drawings of 'William' and 'Ginger' on the cover of Richmal Crompton's famous stories, and quite a few, naturally, looked wide-eyed and tearful. The refreshments, however, seemed to put new life into these timid souls, and, in no time 'T.V.' had his clip-board at the ready to call out the names of pupils and teachers who were to be escorted to their new addresses, 'Leonard, will you take Paul and Jeremy to 5, Idris Villas?' Like a shot, I attended to my duty with Paul and Jeremy asking numerous questions about Tywyn, its inhabitants and their strange language as we made our way through the school gates and down Station Road towards Idris Villas. This was the first of many trips I was to undertake that night, and when it was all over I was glad to see number 18 and bed!

Unlike Summer visitors, the 'Swallows' as my old friend the late Rhydderch Jones called them in his delightful S4C play 'Y WENNOLIAID'; were not on holiday but to carry on as normal a life as possible which included schooling. They joined us at the County using the two 'tin shanties' as we called the annexes. These were occupied by Miss L. C. Roberts, Music, and Miss Gwen Forey, Biology. (I can never think of Miss Forey without recalling the broad smile that lit up the face of my old mate Richard Desmond (Dick) Evans, Gwalia. Every time we came face to face he would smile broadly and say; 'Now put up your hands and tell me . . .' Later, when Dick was still in the Navy and Ifan Hugh Evans and myself were going on holiday to the Isle of Man, we caught up with him in a famous 'Watering hole' in Liverpool. Immediately he saw me, he broke into a smile; 'Put up your hands,' he said 'and tell me, how does a cauliflower prepare for Winter?' He certainly set the tone for our Manx holiday!).

Within a week or so, the excitement of having the evacuees with us died down and life returned to normal. Then, one day, when I returned home from school, I found two strangers sitting in the living room. They were Roy Swift and Stanley Williams — two of Birkenhead's late arrivals! After the initial shock, I must admit that after fourteen or so years on my own, I was pleased to have two 'brothers' with whom to play. We slept in the large front attic bedroom, its dormer window facing Cader Idris and the gas works! Stan and Roy slept in the large double-bed, and I slept in the single.

One Summer evening, Roy produced some cigarettes and we all lit-up — making sure that the window was open. At that precise moment, my grandmother happened to be speaking to Mrs. Hugh Francis Jones next door. 'Good gracious!' said Mrs. Jones, 'I think your attic is on fire!' With that, up came my grandmother, birch-rod in hand, and for some time the only smoke came from the birch-rod in contact with my posterior, I did not smoke again until my office days in Tonfannau.

Before those days, however, there was still some time to go as we prepared for our School Certificate Examination. As there were no air-raid precautions in the school, we, who were not sitting that year were put to the task of digging trenches and filling sandbags. We turned up at the school not in blazers and flannels but in overalls and hob-nailed boots. We found it a pleasant diversion in that beautiful Summer (1940) from studying in stuffy classrooms with the constant aroma of chalk and stale ink, and it was a sad day when the shelters were completed and in use as the school exercised its air-raid drill.

(Alas, our handiwork now lies deep beneath the swimming pool!)

There were air-raid drills, too, in the town when all the Auxiliary Services took part, I was as excited as anyone when the 'bomb' fell in the High Street between the Police Station and Clay's shop and bakery. Sgt. Williams and his companions closed the road as several of us bit-part actors lay prostrate on the highway and on the pavement, a label on our wrist stating our 'injuries' as firemen, air-raid wardens in gas masks, doctors and nurses hurried and scurried to and fro attending to the 'casualties'. My ambition, as I lay outside Marsden's the photographer was to have a ride in one of the ambulances but whatever my 'injuries' they were not bad enough to secure the privilege! Many years later when I did secure the privilege I was wishing with all my being that I was back on the pavement outside Marsden's . . . .

In the crisp early evening air I heard my old friend the Town Hall clock strike six.

I stepped back as Edgar and David Davies arrived with their red Post Office truck loaded with mail bags, Edgar, his cap at the back of his head wished me all the best. Soon, he would be swapping his postman's uniform for that of a 'Jack Tar' telegraphist. 'Don't bend down without making sure that there aren't any dogs behind you!' he said with a broad grin. Edgar never did let me forget a little 'to do' I had one Summer afternoon with his black and white terrier 'Tiger Tim'.

When the tide was out at the New Prom, the rock pools were a joy to behold and the mecca for young children with their jam-jars and nets; of whom, of course, I was one. Crabs and shrimps were the usual haul but very occasionally one would catch the odd lobster and a few prawns. On this particular afternoon my catch was simply a jar of shrimps which I would place on the outside living-room window together with the jar of tadpoles caught in the pond in Sandilands' field. As I proudly made my way home past the bungalow known as: 'The Moorings' I took a short cut through the fields behind avoiding the railway crossing and the long walk back to Idris Villas. As I struggled through the wires at my grandfather's railway-side allotment, I felt a prod in the rear and then the sound of a heart rending tear! I looked in horror as I saw Tim dashing across the railway line towards the Dysynni Wharf with half my trousers in his mouth! To Edgar, it was the source of great amusement as he cheered me through the Wharf with my net and empty jar with Tim wagging his tail in complete contentment!

I had, of course, happier memories of the Dysynni Wharf. Coal trucks from time to time would be shunted — empties taken away to be replaced by full ones. Should I be lucky enough at those times to be playing with Edgar, we were assured of a ride on the foot-plate by kind 'loco' crews from the Machynlleth depot up and down the sidings and, occasionally, as far as the G.W.R., station. As we looked through the circular cab windows we were indeed monarchs of all we could survey.

Other times, when Edgar's father, E. T. Williams, was delivering coal in Bryncrug or Llanegryn he would put us both in the front of the lorry and off we would go — the side windows down with the prevailing wind ruffling our hair, the scent of the blue-bells and primroses adding lustre to the day.

Before the days of the lorry, coal was delivered by horse and cart and the stable now no longer used for its original purpose served as a wood-shed. Here, Tom Roberts, Bobby and Betty's father, on slack days would spend his time chopping logs into firewood. Fed up of playing trains, football or 'tick' (touch) we would drop in on Tom. He was in the territorials or the 'Torriterials' as we used to say, and he used to regale us with stories of parades, exercises and life at the T.A. Summer Camps, with particular emphasis on punishments for misdemeanours. One of the framed pictures on the wall of the Wharf Houses where Edgar lived was: 'The Boyhood of Raleigh' by Sir John Millais. I have often remembered that scene as I thought of Edgar and myself hanging on to Tom's every word.

David Davies looked at me over his glasses, two brown rivulets running down each side of his mouth. Like J. D. Jones, my employer at 'Pretoria', David Davies was an incessant and inveterate chewer of tobacco! 'Remember, Len' he said, 'the way you have been brought up, wherever others go on a Sunday, you know where your duty lies!' Despite his liking for his pint and his tobacco, David Davies was a religious man and an ever-present in 'Ebenezer 'on the Sabbath parading in his bowler hat and black overcoat.

I recalled the number of times I had pushed that truck with him through the High Street and up the sharp incline to the platform to catch the mail train. As my Summer holidays approached, Mr. Benjamin the Postmaster would way lay me as he crossed from the Post Office to his home on the other side of the road, 'Don't forget laddie' he used to say (he always called me 'laddie') 'come and see me in a day or two before school closes and I'll fix you up'. And he always did.

Born and brought up in the town, I knew it well, and so was able to undertake the duties of relief postman in my stride. In those days, the areas were numbered, Town 1, Town 2, Town 3 and so on. As each postman took his fortnight's leave, I would undertake that round. It wasn't long, however, before I got into serious trouble! Having the afternoon off, I would either go fishing or swimming, and so, the sooner I completed my round, the sooner I could engage in my leisure activities! I took over my first round from Ifan Jones, father of Dennis and Jeffrey who lived in Frankwell Street. Everything went well until he returned from leave, and I was about to take over from 'Dei' Ellis whose daughter Buddug was in my class in Pen-y-Bryn. 'Come here you little whipper snapper!' said Ifan Jones 'What do you mean by cutting my throat?' I had no idea what he meant until he explained.

The regulars would take some three hours to undertake the round, their time used up by a cup of tea here, a chat there, (Richard Edwards the shoe repairer was a favourite spot.) a sit down and a smoke yonder, and so, their time was used up nicely! Being only fourteen or fifteen and in the bloom of youth, I would whizz round as quickly as possible in order to finish! 'If he can do it,' mused the authorities, 'why can't you?' I then decided that discretion was the better part of valour and so when I was on High Street, Brynmair, Idris Villas and Sandilands Road I would 'pop' into number eighteen and have a 'cuppa' myself!

It was when I was on this round that Dei Ellis used to say: 'Anything for the penguins today? The penguins were the Nuns who used to holiday in the small cottages over looking the sea between the old and the new proms!

The round I really hated was the one that took me to the Marconi Bungalows, 'Y Faenol', 'Leahurst', 'Rhos-y-dom Cottages', 'Escuan Hall', (with its infamous 'third door' that I used to quiz Meuric so often about in Sunday School!) 'Escuan Isaf', 'Hafoty' and Happy Valley. So far so good but up in the hills there was a farm known as 'Dysyrnant', miles from anywhere. Sometimes, their mail was a farming circular which I religiously delivered to arrive back on the main road on a hot Summer's morning a bath of perspiration.

It was on one of these afternoons that I learnt to swim. Phillip Morgan Jones from Athelestan Road was also working in the Post Office at that time before he joined the R.A.F., and we used to go bathing to the New Prom which, at that time, was a tumble down ruin after one of the worst storms to hit the Cambrian Coast in the early thirties. I remember Eddie Wilson telling me how he stood on the prom as the storm raged, and suddenly he had to move because he could feel the foundations crumbling under his feet. The large boulders, however, formed natural coves for discreet changing. 'Sit on my shoulders' said Phillip one afternoon 'and I'll take you out as far as I can'. Being rather a trusting soul, I obeyed his command. The next moment, I was lashing my arms and feet out for dear life trying to make my way to shore. Phillip had thrown me in headlong! By the time I went home for tea that afternoon I was able to swim!

After tea, it was back to the Post Office to collect my bike, arm-band, mail-bag and 'tablets' (the small white oblong tags containing the number of the box, day and time) to undertake the evening collection from the various boxes which took me from Happy Valley on one side of the town to the railway crossing above 'Sandilands' on the other, and, in between Neptune Hall, the Marine Parade and Beach Road. In just over an hour, I had to be back in the Post Office so that all the letters and cards could be stamped and sorted ready for the evening mail. As more troops were stationed in the various areas, the volume of mail became heavier and many, unable to obtain stamps, posted their letters with coins to cover the postage. My first task, therefore, back at 'base' was to buy stamps and stick them on the unstamped letters.

As six o'clock approached, David Davies and I piled the mail-bags on the truck and made our way to the station. Very often it was a case of 'touch and go'! It was on one of these journeys that David Davies told me that the sad news had reached Tywyn that my boyhood hero had been drowned off the coast of Anglesey. He was P.C. Cledwyn Arthur who had dived into the sea, fully clothed, in a vain attempt to rescue the crew of a Blackburn Botha aircraft which had ditched in the sea off Rhosneigr. (Fifty years later a monument was unveiled at Rhosneigr to commemorate the bravery of P.C. Arthur and his comrades.)

I worshipped 'Cled'. He was in the County before I started school and each day at lunch-time I would watch him and his cousin Basil come down Idris Villas to number 15 for lunch. I watched as they nonchalantly threw their brown school caps at the hat-stand in the hall scoring a direct hit each time! I would then go round the back, and, more often than not, Mrs. Arthur would invite me in to share their pudding — usually apple tart and custard or rhubarb tart and custard. One day, I well remember, there was no pudding left for me, and quite naturally, I felt rather peeved. Seeing a bucket of paste ready for Mr. (George) Arthur and his colleague Mr. David Roberts (Dafydd Roberts Tŷ-Capel) to use that afternoon (they were painters and decorators) I kicked it over in temper! (Forty years later, this 'treacherous' act was to come back to haunt me. Just before my mother and step-father, Mr. & Mrs. George Hughes, left 'Gwermol' for Aberystwyth, I brought my family for a Summer's holiday to Tywyn. Returning from the beach one afternoon, we saw Mrs. Arthur despite her advanced age sitting bolt upright in the front-room window looking like a dowager duchess, her white hair pulled neatly into a bun. She opened the window and I introduced Margaret and David who shook her hand politely. 'Tell me' said Mrs. Arthur 'is Leonard a good father to you?' 'Oh yes' they both said (what could they say as I was standing right there!). 'Well' said Mrs. Arthur, 'I'm going to make him blush now . . .' And out came the story of my 'treachery'!)

Cled was a good footballer, and when Tywyn Celtic in their red and blue strip played at Sandilands Park, it was Cled who marked out the pitch before he played with the team that afternoon. He took me with him on the bar of his bike on both occasions. His cousin Basil lived at 'Hafoty' and often I would be taken on Cled's bike to spend an exciting and entertaining day there. He was a regular member of the School's First XI and I would be there in the school field on the Saturdays they played home against such exciting sides as Ardwyn, Aberystwyth or Barmouth, always running on to the pitch at half-time to talk to my hero. When he joined the Police Force, I must admit, I shed a few tears and made myself a nuisance to Mr. and Mrs. Arthur asking more questions than a Sunday School teacher and cheering wildly when I was told that in a boxing match, Cled had knocked out his opponent in the fourth round at his training college in Manchester. When qualified I was keen to hear of his arrests and delighted to see various photographs of him in uniform. I couldn't wait for him to come home to hear from his own lips the exciting adventures that had befallen him. After what David Davies had said, I was heart-broken to think that Cled would never come home again.

Yes, tragedy had befallen Mr. and Mrs. George Arthur, Enid and Hilda, and of course, Cled's new wife in Anglesey. The joy suddenly went out of Mr. Arthur's life and no more would he pull my leg as of yore.

'Did you go to Sunday School yesterday?' he would ask.

'Yes,' I answered proudly.

'Who's your teacher?'

'Mr. Edward Pugh'.

'Right then' he went on 'who was Samuel's wife?'

I had, of course, no idea. Seeing the look of bewilderment on my face he would say.

'Well Mrs. Edmunds, of course!'

(Samuel Edmunds kept a drapery business on the corner of Church Street opposite 'Star Stores'. In later days, it was the premises of Rhodri C. Davies electrical engineer).

Another of his 'gems' was:

'Who is Jimmy Wilde's father?'

(Jimmy Wilde (1892-1969) the Welsh ghost with a hammer in his hand 'won the world fly-weight title in 1916 and 98 victories inside the distance'. When I met him, he was in his seventies — an immaculate little man in a black 'bowler', navy-blue overcoat and a silk tie decorated with a gold pin).

When I failed to answer, he would laugh and say:

'Ieuan Gwyllt!'

('Ieuan Gwyllt' was the 'nom-de-plume' of the Welsh preacher and hymn-writer, the Rev. John Roberts (1822-1877). 'Gwyllt' is the Welsh word for Wild!!)

If I had forgotten to shave he would say:

'Pity about that ship sunk by a U-boat in the mid-Atlantic. It was carrying a cargo of razor-blades!'

Sometimes, pipe in mouth, cycling by it would be a 'quickie'.

'Did you see that submarine flying over this morning?'

Before I had time to collect my thoughts he was gone. Events had now, however, left the humour far behind. This was also true of many other Tywyn families caught up in world events and one couldn't visit Bob's paper shop, Challoner's Chip Shop,

'Melias', 'Star Supply' and the 'Co-op' without hearing of yet another family in trouble.

(There were local tragedies, too, which touched the hearts of the then closely-knit Tywyn Community. ATS Private Gutteridge committed suicide by jumping from the bedroom window of 'Bryngwalia', her hostel in the High Street. A target-towing 'Hawker Henley' crashed on the banks of the Dysynni killing the pilot, New Zealander, 'Tug' Wilson and in the Happy Valley a 'Wellington' bomber from the R.A.F., stationed at Moreton-in-Marsh, Gloucestershire, never made it home. The sadness and the utter futility was clearly shown in the faces of the carpenters in E. Maengwyn Jones' joinery works; never before had they been asked to prepare for burial so many coffins at any one time.)

Shortly after David Davies told me about Cled, his time of testing came when news broke that his only son, David Lewis, had been killed in the bloody battle for Cassino in Italy. 'He whom the gods love dies young' says the old adage. The gods must have loved so many Tywyn boys . . . .

Five past six. I looked to my right and in the distance I could see a flickering light followed by red-tinged smoke as the fireman shovelled more coal into the 'loco's' hungry furnace in readiness for the gradual gradient between the level crossing — home of the Howells family — and the station

Mr. Dan Williams, the Station Master, came out of his office, stood momentarily when he saw me and then came over to shake my hands.

'Tell Ian I'll write' I said 'and then he'll have my new address'.

Ian, was a year older than myself and in the khaki of the Royal Engineers, down in Hampshire. He was more or less following his civilian occupation in the regiment's rail and transport section. After leaving the County, Ian followed the family tradition by joining G.W.R. as a booking clerk. As I struggled in my School Certificate year, Ian was by the sea in Barmouth and oh, how I envied him when the full panoply of Elstree arrived in the town to film: 'Kipps' the famous novel by H. G. Wells. Yes, Ian had actually sold railway tickets to such world cinema idols as Michael Redgrave, Phyllis Calvert, Diana Wynyard, Michael Wilding and Felix Aylmer! What an honour! When I was at Tonfannau, Ian had moved to Penrhyndeudraeth and on the odd lunch-time I would tell Glenys who was on the 'Bryant's switchboard: 'Go for a cup of coffee to the canteen, Glenys; don't worry about the switch-board, I can manage!' After her footsteps died away in the corridor, I would put my call through to Penrhyndeudraeth Station, and a chat with Ian!

I first met him in Aberdovey when a group of us Tywyn lads one Christmas went to play football against some Aberdovey schoolboys on their recreation ground near the station. A year or so later, I was told that the new Station Master, together with his wife and son, were coming to live to number 16, Idris Villas. The son was, of course, Ian.

As we went to the same school, the same Church and were in the same Sunday School and Band of Hope (where Ian's mother was the Superintendent) we formed a close friendship forged by our love of cycling. At the top of Idris Villas, on the 'Tyddyn Du' side, there was in pre-war days a large sign entitled; 'Places of Interest in the Vicinity' together with their distance from the station a few yards away. On the school holidays and on weekends we would take each in turn and so visit these 'places of interest' — Tal-y-llyn Lake, Llanfihangel-y-Pennant, Bird Rock, Dolgoch

Falls, Castell-y-Bere, Bearded Lake, Llanegryn, Rhoslefain, and so on.

On Summer evenings when homework was done we played cricket in the back between the houses and gardens, and, despite trespassing on numerous flower and vegetable plots, it was our proud boast that we never broke one window! We were also treading a dangerous line and sailing very close to the wind when two of our teachers — Mr. T. V. Davies and Mr. Caradog Williams — lived within a house or two of our pitch! (What was it about Idris Villas that drew so many teachers? I have mentioned Mr. T. V. Davies and Mr. Caradog Williams, then there were Mr. Richard Jones, Miss Gwen Forey, Miss Annie Evans and Miss L. C. Roberts!)

When we felt energetic, we would walk past 'Sandilands Hall' and 'Morfa' farm (pausing to take a look at the bull!) down to the golf links where we would sit in the caddie-shed until one of the locals or visitors would request the pleasure of our company to carry their clubs. We were not entirely 'green horns' at the venture for I had learnt quite a lot from Joe Robson who was the professional at Aberystwyth when I went to the club there on holiday with my Aunt and Uncle who were the caretakers. Ian had also picked up 'snippets' when he visited the more famous Aberdovey club during his residence there. Each round took approxmiately two hours and we were paid 1/6d (7½p). On busy days such as Bank Holidays we had time only for a lime-juice and soda at the clubhouse before venturing out a second time returning home like lottery winners as the gulls made their way up the Dysynni and the cormorant uttered its last cry of the day.

The golf course, so near the river, was fertile ground for wild mushrooms, and often, armed with paper bags we would search diligently for as many as we could find for sale to the visitors. In those days, many houses in Idris Villas kept visitors during the Summer months — the season usually stretching from June to September. Some would board, in other words, rely on the householder to provide them with food for some three pounds a week. Others, for one pound ten shillings (£1.50) would provide their own food, and it was for these people that we earmarked our mushrooms. We were careful, however, not to sell to our own visitors lest the 'takings' be deducted from our pocket money! We therefore presented ourselves at the door of number 14 to sell to the Archers, number 20 to the Thompsons and the Helms in number 23. Mr. and Mrs. Helm later came to live to the town when Mr. Helm retired from the teaching profession, and, in later years, he became our Quarter-master in the Home Guard zealously protecting his wares so that he could account for every cap-badge and button!

Most of Tywyn's visitors came from the Midlands though a fair sprinkling also ventured forth from Lancashire and Yorkshire. The same people came at the same time year in, year out and stayed at the same addresses. To this very day, sixty or more years later, I remember the names of those who stayed with us in 'Gwernol' and my abiding memory of my pre-war Summer schooldays as I set off at eight-forty in the morning is the delicious aroma of bacon sizzling in the pan mixed with the exotic smell of 'Craven A' or 'Passing Cloud'.

My earliest memory, when I must have been some five or six, on rainy mornings was presenting a picture I had drawn to two middle-aged teachers, Miss Adderley and Miss Collins, who came from Manchester. Unable to go to the beach, they would stay in for morning coffee, and, unable to go out to play, I would draw my picture. Every time, it was a case of ten out of ten and a 'Barker and Dobson' butterscotch!

(Alas, at a Bethel Eisteddfod held in the Church House when the drawing of a sailing ship was called for, I failed to get my ten out of ten! The winner was Huw Jones, Athelestan Road who worked in 'Porthgwyn Stores'. Under the nom-de-plume 'Also Tried' he produced a well-crafted sketch of the 'Cutty Sark' in full sail. In fairness, the adjudicator didn't find too much out of place with my effort 'Gwernol' he said: 'Yes, creditable but without any water under it I can't see his ship sailing very far!')

Mr. and Mrs. Knight came from Birmingham. Mr. Knight was an excellent swimmer and many on the 'prom' watched as he swam backwards and forwards with Toby, the Jack Russell, on his back. I was told that as a younger man, he even swam to Aberdovey and back with Toby acknowledging the applause like visiting royalty!

The first man to give me a car ride was the Rev. Hannington who came from Huddersfield. He was a keen fisherman and occasionally he would take me with him to the Broadwater or Tal-y-Llyn Lake. I was to sit quietly, and should I see any fish jumping I was to tell him so that he could cast his fly over the concentric circles before the prey vanished. Feeling sometimes restless and rather bored, I would throw in a stone and shout: 'Over there, Mr. Hannington!' I would then have a good laugh as he tried in vain to rise the non existent fish!

Captain Clarke was the first man I heard speaking Swahili. He, too, was a fisherman and came with his wife and sister-in-law from Chester. One day he was rushed to the Cottage Hospital suffering from acute appendicitis. After a successful operation I went to see him. In the next bed was David Jones 'Dei Erwporthor' — the greengrocer from the High Street. Both Captain Clarke and David Jones had served in East Africa and I found it fascinating to hear them speak Swahili with each another. I spoke English to Captain Clarke and Welsh to David Jones but when they turned to Swahili I was lost!

I can still see David Jones now (although the business later was kept by another Jones, Humphrey, but no relation), standing outside his shop as I sat on the seat outside the station to guide those visitors who had come by train and who requested bed and breakfast in the direction of 18, Idris Villas! (Years later, I often thought of David Jones when the great John Charles bought a sports business in the village of Rhiwbina near my home in Cardiff. 'The Gentle Giant' would stand on the pavement outside his shop talking to all and sundry about his exciting footballing days with Leeds United, Juventus and Wales. Despite his legendary status, he was the most humble of men.)

As the forties approached, the era of the great train visitor was over as more and more cars appeared. When they did come by train I often helped to carry their cases to the station, and saw them off on their great railway adventure to places that were merely names — Liverpool, Manchester, Wolverhampton, Stoke, and Birmingham. Now it was my turn!

How suddenly the time had come! It only seemed a matter of months since I was talking to a young sailor outside the Post Office — not a local boy but someone who had come to visit relatives in the town. (He had come to visit his mother, Mrs. Cambridge, and his brother, Peter. His father, Captain Cambridge, was on the high seas with a local man, Glyn Felix Williams, 'Tywynfa', as his boatswain.) 'If you want to join the Navy' he said; 'don't wait to be called up. If you do, you'll find yourself in the Army, and for a bright lad like yourself that will never do!' It was the first and last time I had the pleasure of his company. Sadly, he lost his life when his ship

HMS *Hood* received an unlucky salvo in the magazine and blew up. It was the incident that blinded Welsh-born actor Edmond Knight who happened to be on the bridge of HMS *Prince of Wales* at the time of the tragedy.

I had the feeling that day, that the young man seemed to be willing me to join the Navy as if he had been overtaken by a premonition of impending doom and wanted to make sure that he had found someone, however inadequate, to take his place. I wasted no time in going to the Labour Exchange in Church Street and requesting the necessary forms from Mr. W. Clarke Roberts. Yes, I was going to volunteer!

In due course I received a letter from the recruiting office in Hill Street, Wrexham, requesting the pleasure of my company for interview, medical examination and intelligence test.. It meant staying in North-East Wales overnight to be bright-eyed and bushy-tailed for my ordeal in the morning. It passed without incident with the usual parting shot; 'We'll let you know'. The Authorities were as good as their word and not only were they kind enough to accept me as a small cog in the great Armada known as the Royal Navy but also gracious enough to give me the day, time and place when they would be pleased to renew my acquaintance . . . .

The train thundered into the station, carriage doors opened and closed noisily, servicemen and a few civilians stepped on and off. Edgar and David Davies hurled in their bags. I jumped on, put my case on the rack above my head, and settled into a corner seat. I suddenly had the urge to get up and look through the window for a last glimpse of the town that had been my home for eighteen years and the treasured memories it held. Guard Aubrey Thomas, still wearing one of his famous roses in his lapel despite the lateness of the year, blew his whistle and changed the colour of his oil-lamp from red to green. Eric, the luggage porter, cast a cursory eye from engine to guard's van to make sure that all doors were firmly closed and with a grunt, a snort and a jolt 'Hinton Manor' slowly pulled out of the station and into the night.

Apart from a brief stop-over in Shrewsbury around midnight for refreshments in the company of my cousin Dewi Mai from Abergynolwyn (He was training to be an aero-engine fitter. He recently retired as Deputy Chief Engineer for 'Dan Air'.) it would be eighteen hours before I reached Plymouth North Road station en route for Torpoint, HMS *Raleigh* and the Royal Navy.